BIBLICALLY BLACK
& BLESSED II

THE CHILDREN OF THE ETHIOPIANS

Henry L. Razor

S.H.E. PUBLISHING, LLC

Biblically Black & Blessed II
Copyright © 2022 by Henry L. Razor.

For information contact :
www.shepublishingllc.com
info@shepublishingllc.com

Book Cover & Title Page Design by Michelle Hudson

ISBN: 978-1-953163-56-1

Edition : December 2022

10 9 8 7 6 5 4 3 2 1

THIS BOOK IS DEDICATED TO the many enlightened individuals who labor for the truth of God's word to be spread abroad upon the face of this earth.

TABLE OF CONTENTS

FOREWORD

I AM EXCITED AND HONORED to write the forward of this second in a series of groundbreaking books. I have read many books on biblical history, but none were as informative and forthright as Biblically Black and Blessed II. I am excited to recommend this book and eager for Black people to learn their purpose. I am also thankful that God has allowed my name to be attached to this magnificent work that will change lives.

Years ago, I purchased Pastor Razor's book Biblically Black and Blessed and could not put it down. I was thrilled with how Pastor Razor did not hold back and gave validated and sourced explanations of the purpose of Black people in God's plan. In his book, Pastor Razor walked readers through the Biblical history of Black people without ignoring historical realities, genealogy, and archeology. Unashamed, Pastor Razor used facts to support his work and showed how vital Black people are to this world. Pastor Razor's approach was trailblazing, and I am excited that Biblically Black and

Blessed II is just as valid, innovative, and essential as the last book.

As a historian, I created The Erudition Network to teach Black History. I have always been passionate about the history of Black people. As a boy, I wanted to know my place and purpose in this world as a Black person. Knowing who you are is crucial because it establishes identity and a sense of value. However, like many Black children, I asked questions and found too few answers. School lessons, family, friends, and even the church could not give me the understanding I sought. I had to trust God and seek answers through study and analysis. I have spent decades studying history worldwide to gain an understanding. Teaching our history is hard; it takes a God-directed mind to stay focused. Pastor Razor kept focused on God's plan by sharing his knowledge in this powerful book.

In the Souls of Black Folks, W.E.B. Du Bois wrote that Black people were behind a veil regarding our place in this world. He hoped that the cover would one day be removed. I affirm that Pastor Razor has removed the veil placed over the assignment, function, and plan for Black people in Biblically Black and Blessed II. Pastor Razor gives the reader a profound understanding of who Black people are to God. He aligns Black people to their assignment and strengthens our bonds with the Israelites without the denigration or ostracism we see in the media. Pastor Razor biblically emphasizes our placement with God and clarifies both nations' assignments.

For decades bigoted Historians chose to refer to Africa as the Dark Continent. African descendants were considered primitive, savage, and unenlightened. Within the last fifty years, honored historians routinely agreed that African History was barbarous and irrelevant to the world. Historians and scientists told lies for bigoted reasons. Due to their falsity, it is a painful fact that most Black people worldwide have been denied their history. Contemporaneously, today's society is bold in its political decrees that teaching Black History in all forms is a criticism, threat, and revision of falsely accepted history.

However, the truth comes from God, and his word will never return void. The truth is that Africans, in the Bible, were called Ethiopians, and they were celebrated in early history. God's hands were all over his people. The facts show that the earliest human remains (Homo sapiens) were found in Ethiopia. The Da'amat society and Aksumite Empires highlight the faith, architectural knowledge, and literate ability of early African society. The ancient military tactics of the Sudanic people continue to be studied in War Academies worldwide. Black people can find our ancestor's tactics and heroism in every major war. You will learn in this book that these were not people without purpose.

In reading Biblically Black and Blessed II, I found myself thinking about these prophetic words written by the famed educator W.E.B. Du Bois in his book Black Reconstruction in America:

"Somebody in each era must make clear the facts with utter disregard to his own wish, desire, and belief. What we have got to know, so far as possible, are the things that actually happened in the world. Then with that much clearer and open to every reader, the philosopher and prophet has a chance to interpret the facts."

Pastor Henry Razor is fulfilling the prayers of our ancestors in Biblically Black and Blessed II. The powerful message in this book is required today. It affirms Black people's purpose without denigrating God's purpose for other nations. Most importantly, Pastor Razor's books ensure that young Black people can find answers to questions about their walk with God. They can hold their heads up, knowing they are God's chosen people with a purpose.

Pastor Razor has prayed, studied, and listened to God. In his first book, he confirmed that we are Biblically Black and

Blessed. This book will show how blessed we are as he illustrates God's Plan for Black People to the world.

Eddie K. Phillips
Public Historian, Founder of The Erudition Network

INTRODUCTION

I GAVE MY LIFE TO CHRIST at a very early age. I traversed through middle school and high school believing that the finished work of Jesus on the cross provided eternal salvation for my soul. My belief is that this finished work would bring me into the presence of God for all of eternity. This knowledge made life refreshing, it provided motivation to overcome obstacles, and it gave me confidence that regardless of what happened on earth, I was destined to spend eternity in a much better place.

Being a young African American Christian was not without challenges. The internal struggle that I experienced because I saw those that claimed Christianity openly practice discrimination was a heavy burden to carry. I often wondered how we could read the same bible, yet live so differently, while claiming to serve the same God. But, without fail, the most frequently entertained question that I received was simply, "where are the black people in the bible?" I have received this question countless times throughout my life. This single question caused me to become a passionate student of the bible, if for no other reason, than to learn where my African ancestors and I are in the plan of God for the world.

I wrote my first book on this topic. In that book, **Biblically Black and Blessed**, I revealed that, according to the Bible, people of African descent were in relationship with God throughout the ages. I demonstrated using the Bible and evidence from noted scientists that people of African descent were the original people and were assigned a purpose by God.

I wrote this book with full understanding of Galatians 3:28:

> *"There is neither Jew nor Greek, there is neither bond nor free, there is neither male nor female: for ye are all one in Christ Jesus."*

This understanding is very important because it emphasizes the biblical fact that God does not view any group of people, or any ethnic nationality of people, to be better than, more important than, or superior to any other group of people on this earth. The biblical fact is that in the words of the Bible, God does not address, separate, or reference any people by race. God, through the pages of the Bible, distinguishes people by nation; more specifically, our nation of origin. I find that in the Bible, people are like pieces of a puzzle. Each piece of a puzzle is distinctly different and fits into the puzzle position that was purposely created specifically for it, so each puzzle piece is therefore required to make the puzzle complete. And because of this, no single piece of the puzzle is more important than the other, because each piece is required in its specific position for the puzzle's completion. The same is true with people. Each nation is distinctly different, but required for successful living on this earth. God created each nation with specific assignments and duties that makes each nation <u>interdependent</u> with the other nations of the world. The success of humanity is dependent upon us accepting, celebrating, and respecting our differences while acknowledging our dependence on each other for the overall success of mankind. Simply put, as the Apostle Paul says in Galatians 3:28, although all nations are distinct and unique, no one nation is more important than the other, we are all one people to God.

Some would dare argue that a book such as this is not important. Others would say that it is divisive and only adds to the problems experienced by the currently existing chasms that separate us today. But my reply to this is that whether we chose to address the reality of who we are per the Bible and the predestined paths identified therein, or ignore it, the Bible will always be right; and it will be proven true regardless. So we are better as people, especially as Believers of God and His word, if we acknowledge the truth of the Bible.

The Bible tells us who we are and from whence we come. It also provides a very detailed description of how we will proceed through life and what our final outcome will be. I learned that when the word of God is rightly divided, we can plainly see the love of God for people of African descent, the responsibility that God placed with the people of African descent, and how the Bible reveals people of African ancestry as God loving and God committed people who are favored by God. The Bible clearly displays God love for **all** people, but the objective of my book is to reveal God's love for and assignment to people of African ancestry, or black people, because we have long been misrepresented in biblical and sacred discourse, or all together omitted from biblical discussions and scholarship.

It has been stated that the best way to understand the Bible is to let the Bible explain itself. This is exactly the way I study the Bible and this is what I will do within the pages of this book. When biblical scripture is connected with understanding, it reveals a truth about Africans and those of African descent that should be a cornerstone of knowledge among all believers, especially believers of African heritage. This book brings to light the often-overlooked fact that

God's relationship with Africans and those of African descent is one of the most cherished, if not the most cherished, relationships that God has with any group of people (nation).

I must emphasize that this book is **not** intended to malign, denigrate, disparage, vilify, bad-mouth, or speak evil of any ethnic group, nationality, or people. But rather, this book emanated and sprang forth from the teachings of Pastor Henry L. Razor and the knowledge gained through a lifetime of study, prayer, and questioning God about the identity of black people. These teachings identify, highlight, and bring into focus the assignment and responsibility that God has placed with people of African ancestry, or black people. It is an assignment that is often dismissed, overlooked, or ignored by many that use the Bible as a guide for living, yet this assignment is critical to the plan of God for all of the earth. This book is intended to be a companion to, or follow up book to Biblically Black and Blessed.

Far too often when the biblical record of Africans, those of African ancestry, or black people is presented; it is first embellished then presented from a position of hate by those whose purpose and goal is to utilize hate for their ungodly purposes. There is no place in the Kingdom of God for hate! This book is not intended or purposed to elevate African or those of African ancestry above any other group or people.

Once again, my understanding of the teachings of the Apostle Paul in Galatians is ever so clear. I will repeat Paul's Galatians 3:28 statement:

> *"There is neither Jew nor Greek, there is neither bond nor free, there is neither male nor female: for ye are all one in Christ Jesus."* **Galatians 3:28 KJV**

Paul teaches us here that in regard to God's relationship with humanity, ethnicity doesn't matter, race doesn't matter, gender doesn't matter; only your acceptance of Christ as savior matters. Peter also explicitly makes it clear that the requirements for pleasing God are consistently and universally applied to all mankind regardless of ethnicity, nationality, or race.

> *"34. Then Peter opened his mouth, and said, Of a truth I perceive that God is no respecter of persons:*
> *35. but in every nation he that feareth him, and worketh righteousness, is accepted with him."* **Acts 10:34-35 KJV**

Peter teaches us that God accepts, from every nation, those that fear (*reverence*) Him and works righteousness. But it must be noted that Peter states "*in every nation*". With this phrase Peter makes us aware of a point that must not be overlooked. There are many nations, not a single nation. God did not create a single people with a single functional purpose for the benefit of humanity. He created multiple nations that make humanity and the world better when we love each other, respect each other, and work together in the Love of God. We must acknowledge that although we are unique, and thereby different, THERE ARE NO SUPERIOR NATIONS OR SUPERIOR PEOPLE IN THIS WORLD! In acknowledging this, we must then seek to understand how each of us has an equal part in the advancement of humanity. This is important because, just as there are many parts of the human body and each part is unique with its specific purpose, there are many nations that comprise the world and these nations also have specific purposes. So understanding God's assignment to any nation is foundational in understanding God's purpose for that people.

So the question one might ask is, "if we are all one before God, then why write a book about any specific nation or people?" This book is written because truth of the scripture must be known, understood, and implemented for us to please God. We are not all of the same earthly nation. God did not implement the nations of this world in this manner. We have differences that should be celebrated. Our differences are what make the world the great place of human existence. Our differences don't make us inferior or superior to others, but rather they make us depend and rely on each other for the existence of mankind. Because we are different, God has different purposes for us and when those purposes work together in unison, the world becomes a place where God's kingdom is the established authority, just like it is in Heaven. This is exactly what Jesus commanded us to pray for.[1]

In this book I will examine the words of Jesus in St. John 10:16. When these words are taken into context with other scripture, I believe that they reveal a love for Africans, and those of African ancestry, that God wanted the world to know and understand. These words also help in the realization that just as God has a purpose for the Israelites, He also has a purpose for Africans and those of African ancestry. These words should become a cornerstone of teaching in all churches and believers of African descent should use this book to create a foundation of faith, knowledge, and love of God in our community at large.

I currently serve as Senior Pastor of Faith Hope & Charity Ministries in Chicago, Illinois. The intent and purpose of this book and all of my Black History Month teachings are to highlight the rich spiritual heritage of black people while identifying and celebrating the long-standing relationship that black people enjoy with God.

I wrote the first Biblically Black and Blessed by request of my church after teaching for years, during Black History Month, about God's relationship with people of African

---

[1] Matthew 6:10 KJV

ancestry. The first book focused on the relationship that God has established with black people. That book was only purposed to be distributed to the members of our church. But after numerous requests from others, I transferred it to a local publisher and had it released through publishing distribution channels. This book digs deeper into this relationship and shows, using scripture as the basis and support, that black people are indeed God's people; and just like the nation of Israel, God has made divine assignments to black people on this earth. This book uses scripture to show that the Bible has always supported black people as God's people and the divine assignment given to black people is necessary for God's Kingdom to be established on the earth.

This book does not demonize any nation, group, or people. Nothing about this book diminishes or negates the assignment and responsibility that God has placed with the people of Israel. For truly the Bible is clear on God's relationship with the house of Israel, His call for them to be His people, and His assignment to them on the earth. But what this book does is that it uses scripture to show that black people are also God's people; it shows that black people also have an assignment from God and if God's kingdom is to be established on earth, black people must complete their divine assignment.

The purpose of this book is to prepare, not only black people, but all people, to acknowledge, accept, and fulfill our divine assignments so that God's kingdom can be established "*on earth as it is in Heaven*" and the glorious harmony of Heaven will permeate throughout the nations of the world.

I don't know if any future Biblically Black and Blessed books will follow, I will write as God leads me via the Holy Spirit. For apparent reasons, this book, as well as the first **Biblically Black and Blessed**, have focused on God's relationship with, and His assignment to, Black people on the earth. I have highlighted these points with comprehensive biblical support, but more importantly, I have done this without denigrating, disparaging, berating, or attacking any other people, nation, group, etc. I have gone to great lengths to respect God's relationship with other nations while highlighting God's relationship with, and His assignment to black people.

I pray that this book motivates and persuades you to love and live in harmony with your neighbor, acknowledge your divine assignment from God, and through your life's purpose, make this world a much better place to live. I believe that this book will grab your attention and focus. As you read this book, I strongly encourage you to follow and read each of the biblical references that are noted at the bottom of the pages. As you follow these references, you will conclude that the message of this book is biblical, revealing both the intent and plan of God for black people on this earth.

II

Biblical Sheep

Know ye that the LORD he is God:
it is he that hath made us, and not we ourselves;
we are his people, and the sheep of his pasture.
Psalms 100:3

I've always thought the biblical likening of humans to sheep to be an interesting paradigm. Of all of the animals that are mentioned in the Holy Scriptures, what makes humanity appear to God as sheep? Sheep are mentioned in the Bible more than 500 times, appearing much more frequently than any other animal. I now understand that the prominence of sheep in the Bible grows out of two realities. First, sheep were important to the nomads and agricultural life of people during biblical times. This would mean that almost everyone in biblical times would understand any parable, paradigm, or proverbs that used sheep as a central character. Secondly, sheep being used throughout the Bible to symbolically refer to God's people makes a powerful statement about the dependence of believers on our supernatural shepherd. This is the very first realization that I noticed; not all humans are referred to as sheep in the bible. Only the people that respond to God's love by accepting Him as savior and pressing into the kingdom of God are referred to as sheep. Others are referred to as goats,[2] whereas others are referred to as wolves[3]. It becomes ever so clear that the sheep and the goats are separated. And this separation is based on whether a person accepts, honors, and serves the Lord (sheep), or not (goats). So, to understand why God consistently refers to those that

---

[2] Matthew 25:33
[3] Matthew 7:15

15

acknowledge, accept, honor, and serve Him as sheep, we will look at the natural characteristics of sheep.

Characteristics of Sheep

Sheep must be led because they have no sense of direction. This simply means that sheep require a shepherd for survival. They are totally dependent upon their shepherd for the necessities of life. Farmingbase.com states that *"Without a shepherd, sheep are prone to wandering off from the flock and there's a reason for this. Naturally, sheep are hotwired to follow each other."*[4] Without a shepherd, sheep will play follow the leader (follow the sheep closest to them that is in front of them). And since the leading sheep has no idea where it is going, the following sheep will almost always scatter or be led into danger and destruction. Jesus alludes to this characteristic of sheep in Matthew 9:36:

> *"But when he saw the multitudes, he was moved with compassion on them, because they fainted, and were scattered abroad, as sheep having no shepherd."*

As Jesus journeyed through cities and villages, teaching in the synagogues, healing and helping the people of His day, He acquired a huge following of people desperately in need.

---

[4] https://farmingbase.com/can-sheep-live-without-a-shepherd/

16

The scripture above references a specific occasion, where Jesus stopped and observed the crowd. I'm sure that there would be sick people in the crowd, as were people with financial problems, people with family problems, depressed people, people at the end of their rope, etc. They all had heard of Jesus and were willing to take a chance that He could assist them in the area of their life where they needed help. When you are ministry focused in your heart, you realize that ministry is all about serving. It's about alleviating the heavy burdens of those that are being crushed while trying to carry their burden. It's about bringing calm to those that are filled with anxiety. It's about bringing hope to those that are depressed. It's about relieving the pain of suffering. So seeing so many anxious people in need moved Jesus to compassion. These sheep needed a shepherd!

The shepherd is given the responsibility of watching over the sheep and safely leading them to their destination. This is a good time to define the word '*flock*' as related to sheep. A flock is defined as a group of like animals assembled or herded together under the guidance of one leader. So by referring to believers as 'His sheep', God is saying that believers are under His guidance and leadership.

It has also been stated that once sheep are within a flock and under the leadership of a shepherd, they know that shepherd's voice and can recognize it even in the midst of multiple people speaking. So all the shepherd has to do is call, and all of his sheep will acknowledge his call and come forward. Sheep that are under a different shepherd's leadership will also hear the call, but they won't recognize the voice, and hence they will not acknowledge the call and they will not come. This is definitely a characteristic that Jesus refers to in John 10:4-5

> *4. And when he putteth forth his own sheep, he goeth before them, and the sheep follow him: for they know his voice.*
> *5. And a stranger will they not follow, but will flee from him: for they know not the voice of strangers*

The second characteristic of sheep that I must mention is that sheep are innocent and defenseless. They have almost no ability to defend themselves from predators. For their protection, they rely wholly upon their shepherd. Before David was king, he was responsible for shepherding his father's sheep.[5] He mentions to King Saul that while watching the sheep, a lion, and a bear, came upon the flock and took a sheep with intentions of feasting on it. But it was David's job as the shepherd to protect the sheep, so he grabbed the lion by the beard and secured the sheep. When the lion turned on him, he said *"and when he arose against me, I caught him by his beard, and smote him, and slew him."* David as the shepherd of his father's sheep placed

---

[5] 1 Samuel 17:34

himself between the sheep and danger because he realized that the sheep were docile, innocent, and defenseless creatures that depended on him for safety and safe passage. Jesus takes this even further when he says in John 10:11

"the good shepherd giveth his life for the sheep"

Because of the defenseless nature of sheep, it is important that the shepherd be a person of character that can be trusted to put the safety of the sheep first. Jesus contrasted a good shepherd with one that was just doing the job for the money, or as Jesus referred to them, hirelings. Jesus says in John 10:12-13

> *" 12. But he that is an hireling, and not the shepherd, whose own the sheep are not, seeth the wolf coming, and leaveth the sheep, and fleeth: and the wolf catcheth them, and scattereth the sheep.*
> *13. The hireling fleeth, because he is an hireling, and careth not for the sheep."*

A shepherd is simply someone who shepherds, or cares for, God's flock. In our churches today we typically call them pastors. I must take a moment here to emphasize how important it is that you select a worship assembly (church) with a shepherd that places your safety, security, and advancement as a priority. The character, outlook, and perspective of the shepherd that's leading the church should be a primary consideration when deciding to become a member of any church. Note that the pastor is a local shepherd, and the congregants of the church that he/she leads would be a local 'flock'. It is important that the pastor NOT be a hireling!

The third characteristic that I will mention should encourage any and every believer in our daily walk. I want you to think about this question. Have you ever seen a sheep being used to carry anything? Sheep are not created to carry a burden (load). Horses, mules, elephants, lions, dogs, etc. can carry loads, push or pull loads, and be used as living work machines. But not sheep! Sheep must give their load to their shepherd and it's the responsibility of the shepherd to figure out how to transport that load. Isn't this just like God. Once we are within His flock, He doesn't want us to concern ourselves with the heavy burdens that life presents so he tells us to give them to Him and let Him handle them. In Psalms 55:22, God says

Cast thy burden upon the LORD, and he shall sustain thee:

Other animals are valued because of their ability to carry, pull, or push a load. Sheep too, are valuable, but their value is assessed in other ways. And carrying a burden is not an indication of value in sheep. The contributions of sheep assist us in being sustained in this world. Wool for a protective warm covering and milk for nourishment are just a couple of the valuable contributions of sheep. I live in Chicago where the cold and wind can be deadly during the winter season. But the warmth provided by wool garments makes even the harshest environmental elements sustainable for periods of time. I thank God for a shepherd that has directed me to give Him my burdens, so I'll just provide the value to humanity that I, as a believer, was created to provide. I will live out my purpose with complete confidence in the shepherd and allow the Lord (my shepherd) to lift every heavy burden from me.

Some have arrived at a conclusion that sheep will simply follow anyone with any message regardless of the truth, soundness, or viability of that message. This is not true. As earlier stated, sheep learn the voice of their shepherd and respond in the affirmative only when they hear that voice. At the core of our existence is that we were all created by God. We all belong to God[6]. God's desire is that we all accept His finished work, and thereby be the sheep of His pasture. We were created for this purpose. This means that we were created with an innate predisposition to follow the Lord, thereby acknowledging Him as our Shepherd. We were born with a God nature that inherently desires to please the Lord, who is the shepherd. So God created us to be His sheep.

---

[6] Ezekiel 18:4

I believe that I must take a few lines of this book and provide some explanation and clarity around my statement that we were born with an innate pre-disposition to serve God. I have heard so many people explain the unGodly, immoral, or unethical character of others as the result of man being born with a sin nature. This is something that I vehemently disagree with, simply because we are created in God's image. Sin is not natural for God, in God, or by God. I believe that the Bible goes to great lengths to show that sin is a result of evil influence, not the inherent nature of man. From the very beginning, sin was <u>not</u> something that man did naturally, but man sinned by yielding to the influence of Satan. I believe that the most powerful biblical proof of this is found in Romans 2:14

> *"For when the Gentiles, which have not the law, do by nature the things contained in the law, these, having not the law, are a law unto themselves"*

Here the Apostle Paul explains that when the gentiles, who were evil people, obey their nature, they do the righteousness that is contained in the law; with their natural obedience, their actions then become a law unto them. But the point made here is how they arrive at obedience. They do it *"by nature"* or naturally. So even without acknowledging The Lord as your shepherd or submitting to His guidance and laws, the inherent nature of man is to perform the works of our creator. But this becomes a nearly impossible task because of the influence of sin. Saul struggled with this prior to his Damascus Road conversion. He wrote about it in Romans 7:19

> *"For the good that I would I do not: but the evil which I would not, that I do."*

Paul indicates that he wants to do right, but sin influences him to do what's not right. The influence of sin is a powerful force. A force of such power and persuasion that Christ has to be accepted to experience victory over it.[7]

Now back to the sheep. Some have reasoned that sheep are dumb. But this reasoning is actually far from the truth. Sheep are really intelligent creatures that understand from whom their help and hope comes. They are trusting creatures that place confidence in the leadership of their shepherd; on whom they depend and rely for direction, guidance, nourishment, protection, safety, and any other life's needs that they may have. So considering the characteristics of sheep, and the responsibility of a shepherd, it's no wonder that God likens believers to sheep that are under His care, His guidance, His leadership, and His protection. He wants His sheep to have every confidence in His provision. David

---

[7] Romans 8:2

said "The Lord is my shepherd, I shall not want"[8]. It's reassuring to know that as the Lord's sheep, we have a shepherd that provides our every need. Just consider the functions that David, in Psalm 23, said the shepherd performed for him:

- He sufficiently provides so that I have no want (*I shall not want*)
- He makes me rest in comfortable well supplied pastures (*lie down in green pastures*)
- He leads me to calmness (*still waters*)
- He re-energizes & reinvigorates me (*restores my soul*)
- He leads me in the right direction (*paths of righteousness*)
- He takes away the fear of life-threatening dangers (*yea, though I walk through the valley of the shadow of death, I will fear no evil*)
- He stays with me to protect me (*Thou are with me*)
- He comforts me (*Thy road and they staff*)
- He makes sure that I am nourished even in the sight of those that seek to destroy me (*prepares a table in the presence of my enemies*)

---

[8] Psalms 23:1

- He lets everyone know that I am blessed and highly favored (*anointest my head with oil*)
- He gives me more than enough (*cup runneth over*)
- He provides the visible evidence of His blessings upon me (*goodness and mercy shall follow me all the days of my life*)
- He gives me a place to reside safely forever (*I shall dwell in the house of the Lord forever*)

O what a shepherd! It is such an honor and blessing to be in the care of such a wonderful shepherd. This is the blessing of being one of God's sheep.

II

BELIEVE THE BIBLE

Study to shew thyself approved unto God,
a workman that needeth not to be ashamed,
rightly dividing the word of truth.
2 Timothy 2:15

T he picture used at the bottom of this page is the logo for Bible Class at our local church. Our Bible class is framed by my philosophy for reading and studying the Bible. It is a very simple philosophy that must be accompanied with prayer. I study the Bible to obtain understanding of God's purpose for mankind and His creation, as well as His expectation of me and how I can live in such a way that He finds me pleasing. My Bible study philosophy is simple, but powerful and purposeful. It is simply this:

BELIEVE WHAT THE BIBLE SAY INSTEAD OF TRYING TO MAKE THE BIBLE SAY WHAT YOU BELIEVE.

This is a powerful method of studying God's word that will yield knowledge and understanding that God, Himself, will confirm. But as powerful as this method is, I have found that it is utilized by very few people. We all have arrived at this point in our life from somewhere. It is this 'somewhere' that usually defines how we understand the scriptures. We come from denominations, churches, religious institutions, etc. that have shaped how we view God's word. The shaping of our views by our past is so powerful that I've heard people read a verse, then start their explanation by saying "this is what this verse is really saying". But when you simply believe what the Bible says, you understand that God is more knowledgeable, more intelligent, and has more understanding than any of His creation, so He knows exactly how to say what He means. So many times, we bring what we have been told that the Bible says into our Bible study, even when the verses that we are studying don't match what we were told that they mean. And let's be real, many in my generation were taught the Bible by well-meaning people that were not highly educated. They did the best that they could do with the education and learning that they had. But if we are truthful, we have to acknowledge that they misunderstood many of the things that they were reading in the Bible. And rather than make and apply the corrections to their teachings, so many in my generation have continued propagating their erroneous teachings for various reasons. It is well understood that God does not change, His requirements doesn't change, and His word doesn't change. But our understanding changes, our knowledge increases, and educational advances allow us to arrive at a better understanding of what the words, sentences, and verses of the Bible mean. I grew up in the Earle COGIC in Earle Arkansas. It was a lively and spirit filled church in the Mississippi Delta. The chairman of the deacon's board during my childhood was a deacon named Christopher C. Alexander. Deacon C.C. Alexander was a driving force in me arriving at my Bible study philosophy. He would often say to me "Bro. Razor, you have an opportunity that we did not have. You can go to school, get an education, and use that education to study the Bible. Take advantage of this opportunity". He constantly reminded me that they had very little formal education so it was a struggle to know and understand the verses as well as I could if I applied what I learned in school to my Bible study. Whenever I was at church, he made me read; either the opening scripture, read for the preacher, or whatever that needed to be read. I can remember times when he was reading from the YPWW book and the lessons were in the Old Testament. Those Old Testament verses contain a lot of names that are hard to pronounce. He would call me up and tell me to read those verses. He said openly that he wanted me to call those names out and pronounce them using the pronunciation methods that I had learned in school. My biological father didn't live with us in our home and my mother never really showed an interest in my schooling, but Deacon Alexander and the other older church members checked on my schooling, my grades, and my progress. And they always let me know that they wanted me to use my education to arrive at a better understanding of God's word, God's will, and God's requirement for mankind.

I mention my method and philosophy for studying the Bible because this book would not be possible without that method. And if you have read any of my previous books, you know that they are all based on scripture as scripture is written, and not merely what I believe. I always "*believe what the Bible says*" instead of trying to make the Bible "*say what I believe*". So as I get into the core of this book, I ask that you believe what the Bible says, as opposed to trying to make the Bible say what you believe. I believe that when you do this, the following pages of this book will come alive to you and your understanding of God's purpose for the children of Israel (*those of Jewish ancestry*), the children of the Ethiopians (*those of African ancestry*), and the entire world will increase immensely.

II

GOD'S OTHER SHEEP

*And other sheep I have, which are not of this fold: them
also I must bring, and they shall hear my voice; and there
shall be one fold, and one shepherd.*

John 10:16

With this statement Jesus provided insight into the relationship that God has with two nations that proceeded from the sons of Noah. But first let's closely examine the words of Jesus here and the environment in which He spoke these words, and then we will identify the two nations spoken of.

We know that when Jesus made these statements, He was talking directly to the Jews because John 10:19 states:

> *19. There was a division therefore again among the Jews for these sayings*

We have shown in earlier chapters of this book that sheep are believers that follow the Lord, or as David said, believers that acknowledge the Lord as their shepherd. And since a sheepfold is a shelter or house for a flock of sheep, the words that Jesus speaks here are very revealing regarding relationships that existed between God and His sheep.

Speaking directly to the Jews, Jesus said "other sheep I have." And since I have already explained that sheep are people, Jesus is telling the Jews that He has other people. But then he finished this statement by saying that these other sheep "are not of this fold". So Jesus emphasizes to the Jews that His other people are not part of their house; they are not a part of their shelter; they are not a part of their sheepfold;

they are not part of Israel. In other words, the other people (*sheep*) that belong to God are not Jews!

Take a Moment and Let That Sink In!

Throughout the Bible, God repeatedly referred to Israel as the 'house of Jacob' or the 'house of Israel'.[9] So truly in the eyes of God, Israel were His sheep and where He placed them (*their house or their nation*) is their sheepfold. So, for Jesus to come into that sheepfold (nation) and declare that God has other sheep (people) that are not in this fold (that are not Jews) had to be an eye opening statement to the Jews.

I want to emphasize here that neither Jesus nor I are saying that the Jews are not God's people. As a matter of fact, Jesus was stating just the opposite. He **was** saying that the Jews are God's people, but He is also meticulously emphasizing that the Jews are not God's **only** people. He wanted them to know that God has other sheep, (other people) that are not of their fold (that are not Jews).

I also want to emphasize that neither Jesus nor I are negating the responsibility that God has placed with the Jewish people. It will become ever so clear, after we

---

[9] Jeremiah 31:27; Matthew15:24; Isaiah 14:1; Isaiah 46:3

understand Jesus' statement here, that the Jews were called, selected, and appointed by God for specific priestly duties upon this earth. And this assignment must be carried out by them, and no one else but them. God will not change His mind; they must do what God selected them to do.[10] But what the words of Jesus also say to us is the fact that God has other people, who are not Jews, which He has also placed responsibility with. In my book **Biblically Black and Blessed**, I give detail on the assignment and responsibility that God has given to the African descendents of Noah's son Ham. Now we clearly see that one of the nations referenced by Jesus in John 10:16 is the Jews. Jesus had entered into their sheepfold and was speaking directly to them when He stated that He has other sheep that are not of their sheepfold. When I explain this to people, I always get the question: *"who then are God's other sheep?"*

In my previous book, **Biblically Black and Blessed**, I take the time to look at the works of the descendents of Noah's son Ham and how God consistently assigned them the responsibility of nurturing, protecting, providing for, and fighting for Israel whenever Abraham, Jacob, Jesus, or the nation Israel were in trouble. In that book, I show that the functional duties of the descendants of Ham represent God assignment to them and God's purpose for them, just as the

---

[10] Romans 11:29

functional messenger responsibilities represented God's assignment to and purpose for the archangel Gabriel. But in identifying this other nation referenced by Jesus with his statement regarding His other sheep, I will go directly to the prophet Amos and show that the other sheep (other nation) is clearly identified. Amos 9:7 reads:

> *Are ye not as children of the Ethiopians unto me, O children of Israel? saith the LORD. Have not I brought up Israel out of the land of Egypt? and the Philistines from Caphtor, and the Syrians from Kir?*

In this one verse God asks Israel a rhetorical question: *"are ye not as the children of the Ethiopians unto me"*. It is rhetorical because God knows the answer, He wants Israel to acknowledge and accept the answer, and it's a question for which he also provides proof that the answer must be affirmative (yes). So if Israel is '*God's people*', and their relationship with God is just like the Children of the Ethiopians, then God is saying that **the children of the Ethiopians are also His people**! So when Jesus makes the statement about God's other sheep (people), who are not Jews, then according to the prophet Amos, the children of the Ethiopians would be those other people. But who are the children of the Ethiopians? Let's take a detailed look.

The word "*Ethiopian*" was a Greek term used to identify black-skinned people in general, and the word was applied

38

to Cush (or sometimes represented as Kush) and his descendants (the Cushites were well known to the Hebrews and often mentioned in the Hebrew Bible).[11] According to Sampson S. Ndoga of the University of Pretoria in South Africa, "Ethiopia is mentioned variously in every major division of the Hebrew Bible and used interchangeably with Cush, and it was later identified with Nubia and Aksum. In its broader sense, the name Aethiopia (*Ethiopia*) should not be equated with Ethiopia of today which was designated in 1885. **All the lands south of the Sahara or inhabited by black people represent the vast extent of ancient Ethiopia**". This association of ancient Ethiopia with the whole of Africa or 'Cush' is validated and verified by numerous archaeologists and historians.[12]

---

[11] Wikipedia

[12]https://biblicalstudies.org.uk/pdf/ajet/18-2_143.pdf;
https://www.asor.org/anetoday/2020/12/cushites-hebrew-bible/

The Continent of Africa with the Sahara in Grey

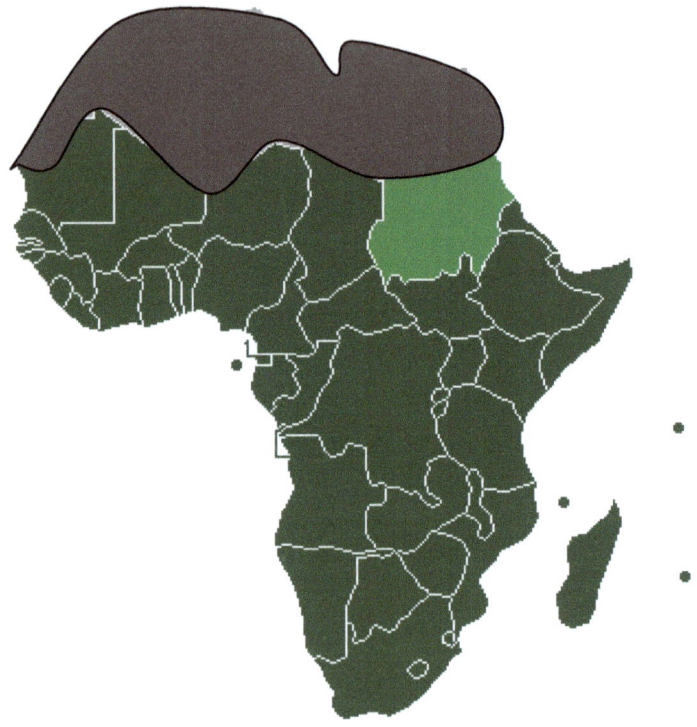

Above is the continent of Africa with the Sahara depicted in grey[13]. Biblical Ethiopia existed as all of the land mass south of the Sahara. This shows that biblical Ethiopia was the overwhelming majority of the African continent and the biblical Ethiopians represented the overwhelming majority of the African people.

---

[13] Wikipedia -- https://en.wikipedia.org/wiki/Sub-Saharan_Africa#/media/File:Sub-Saharan_Africa_definition_UN.png

Now take a look at the middle passage routes that are historically documented and verified as the routes used to bring Africans to the western nations and force them into slavery.[14]

---

[14] **Adaobi Tricia Nwaubani** – Nigerian Journalist "My Nigerian great-grandfather sold slaves"

The Transatlantic Slave Trade

Captives taken from Africa to the Americas and Europe, 16th-19th Century

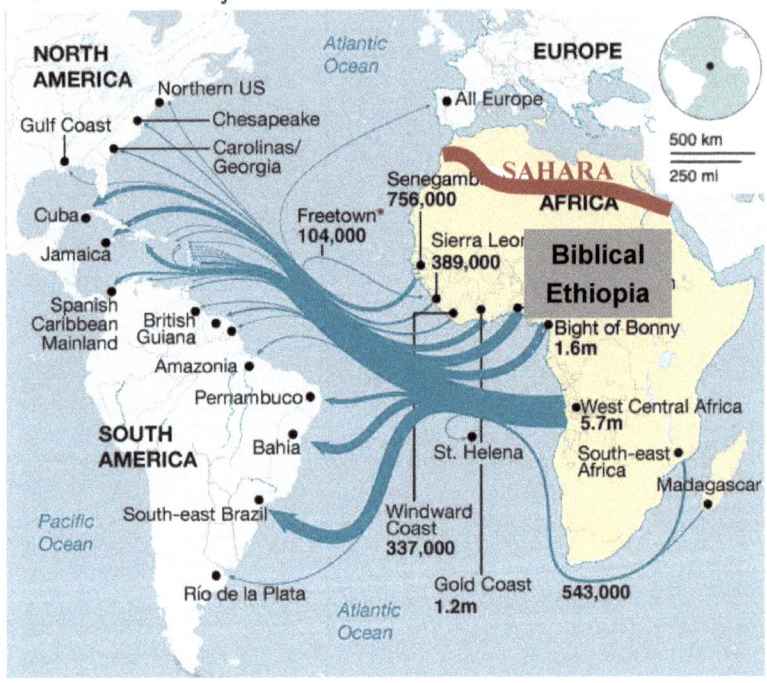

The very first fact that these maps show is that the trip from Africa to the Americas for the Africans who were forced into slavery originated in Biblical Ethiopia, as its boundaries are defined in the bible. Keep in mind that the current nation of Ethiopia as we know it today, with its current boundaries, was not defined until 1885 when the European nations divided the African continent for colonization.[15] Prior to this, the entire land mass south of the Sahara was generally referred to as Ethiopia. (Some historians have equated the entire continent of Africa with Biblical Ethiopia during that time, but since the Bible regularly names Egypt (Mizraim) and Cyrene (Phut) independently of Ethiopia, I use sub-Saharan Africa in this book to represent Biblical Ethiopia). That pre 1885 sub-Saharan African land mass is Biblical Ethiopia. So the current nations of Nigeria, Sudan, The Congo, Zimbabwe, and every current nation positioned below the Sahara were all a part of Biblical Ethiopia. Since the first Africans who would be slaves began arriving on the North American continent in 1619, they would have been kidnapped from what was Biblical Ethiopia. This would make the black people in North America, South America, and the Caribbean Islands direct descendents of the Ethiopians of the Bible. Therefore, the overwhelming majority of black people

---

[15] Nations online map --
https://www.nationsonline.org/oneworld/map/africa-historical-map-1885.htm

currently residing in the United States, and in the western hemisphere, are of Biblical Ethiopian heritage. Therefore, Black people in America, along with the people of sub-Saharan Africa are the 'children of the Ethiopians' that God mentions in Amos 9:7. And these Black people are the people of whom God refers when He tells the Jewish people that they are like the 'children of the Ethiopians'. We, as black people with Biblical Ethiopian heritage, should be proud of our relationship with God. All indications in the pages of the Bible are that we were first in relationship with God, and as you will see in the later pages of this book, our relationship with God has never been broken or severed. God has provided proof to the Jewish people that to Him, they are like the Ethiopians. WOW! God views His relationship with the Ethiopians as special and dear.

As stated in my earlier book, ***Biblically Black and Blessed***, the word Ethiopia means 'burnt face' or black skinned. It was the land that produced the ***Queen of Sheba***[16] who traveled to Israel to validate the wisdom of Solomon before she endorsed him; this land also produced ***King Tirhakah***[17] who traveled to deliver Israel from what would have been certain Assyrian destruction; it was also the land that the Ethiopian Eunuch[18], who Phillip introduced to Jesus,

---

[16] 1 Kings chapter 10
[17] 2 Kings 19:9
[18] Acts 8:26-40

called home. So we must not think of Biblical Ethiopia as the current day Ethiopia, but rather Biblical Ethiopia embodies the homeland of all of the dark skinned people that were indigenous to the African continent. So we see that in Amos 9:7, God is driving home the point that the children of Israel are just as the children of the Ethiopians to Him. Let this sink in.

GOD IS TELLING THE CHILDREN OF ISRAEL THAT TO HIM, THEY ARE JUST LIKE THE CHILDREN OF THE ETHIOPIANS.

And if making this statement was not enough, God goes even further by making reference to the many great exploits and deliverances that He did for Israel. He listed these great acts as proof that they were to Him like the Ethiopians. God tells Israel that His delivering them out of Egypt, His delivering them from the Philistines, and His delivering them from the Syrians is the proof that He has treated them just as He had treated the Ethiopians. Since the mighty acts of God are the proof, then one can only marvel and wonder at what great works God did for the Black people of African descent (the Ethiopians). Now you see that when Jesus makes the statement that He has "*other sheep*" who are not Jews, He is referring to the same people that God identified in Amos 9:7, the Black people of Africa. This makes a phenomenal point about God's relationship with Africans and those of African ancestry. Once again I must state that the fact that Africans are God's people in no way negates the personage of the Jews; nor does it diminish the priestly duties and responsibilities assigned to them as a nation; neither does it imply that they are not God's people; what this does is that it identifies God's other people (*other sheep*), and further examination will reveal God's assignment to His 'other people' (Africans and those of African ancestry). I identify that assignment by function and explain it in my book '*Biblically Black and Blessed*'. One final point on Amos 9:7, if those miraculous deliverances are proof that to God, the Children of Israel are as the Children of the Ethiopians, then God would have already performed miraculous acts for the Children of the Ethiopians. This would have placed the Ethiopians in relationship with God prior to Israel entering into their relationship with God.

Since the Ethiopians have now been identified as the 'other sheep' that Jesus spoke of, and sheep have been defined as people that follow their shepherd, then the Ethiopians would have been following God before Jesus came into this world, because Jesus states that they are His sheep. He doesn't say that they will become His sheep, but they are already His sheep. This forces us to closely examine the scriptures relative to the spirituality of biblical Africans.

When speaking of the spirituality of the Biblical Ethiopians, most theologians and historians simply say that they were polytheistic, or they worshipped multiple Gods. However, after closely examining the scriptures that relate to Biblical Ethiopians, I find that to ascribe polytheism to them is an error. Whether this error was mistakenly innocent or maliciously purposeful is the question that immediately consumes me when this subject arises in conversation. In my previous book, Biblically Black and Blessed, I explain, with biblical support, that the Biblical Ethiopians (indigenous Africans) have always served the only true God. We must understand that until God revealed Himself to Moses, no nation on the earth knew God as God. They simply knew that a Supreme Being existed that was responsible for creating and controlling the things for which they had no power themselves to control. The Apostle Paul said that even nature reveals this Supreme Being.[19] So the Biblical Ethiopians created figures of gold, silver, stone, or other statues to represent the Supreme Being of whom they had no knowledge. They were not worshipping these images as God; they were using these images to represent the Supreme Being. And God, understanding that they had no knowledge of Him, accepted this because He knew that they were ignorant of who He was.[20] However, once knowledge of God

---

[19] Romans 1:20
[20] Acts 17:29-30

was in the earth, available, and accessible, God no longer accepted this form of worship and He no longer overlooked this ignorance. Today, God requires all men everywhere to repent and enter into a relationship with Him. We see the example of this when Phillip shared his knowledge of Jesus with the Ethiopian Eunuch.[21]But even prior to this, whenever God called upon His Biblical Ethiopian sheep, they willingly answered His call.[22]We know of the salvation that God wrought through Tirhakah, King of Ethiopia, or the validation of Solomon that God provided through the Queen of Sheba. But consider the salvation of Jeremiah the prophet that God provided through Ebed-melech the Ethiopian.[23] He risked his life by standing up to the King and speaking against the unjust imprisonment of Jeremiah. After hearing Ebed-melech the Ethiopian, Jeremiah was released and his life spared. The scriptures are clear that every time that God called upon the Biblical Ethiopians, they were there to function in the area of their Godly assignment. The Bible provides documented proof that Biblical Ethiopians (indigenous Africans) have always served the true and living God! And this service to God was never in doubt, as God rewarded them with wealth, power, and prestige that made them the envy of the world. This service to the Supreme Being was satisfying to God until Jesus came.

---

[21] Acts 8:26-40
[22] 2 Kings 19:8-9; 1 Kings 10; Jeremiah 38:7-13
[23] Jeremiah 38:7-13

When God selected Israel to be His nation of priests[24], the very first thing that He did was reveal Himself to them as God.[25] Then their assignment as God's priests on the earth had two primary and distinct functions:

1. They were to reconnect the Gentiles back to God
2. They were to identify God as the Supreme Being to the Biblical Ethiopians

Israel never completed these assignments. They continually and consistently failed. And as long as Israel failed in their priestly duties, the spirituality of the Biblical Ethiopians was accepted by God as they continued to worship the Supreme Being with their statues of stone, sticks, stubble, etc. that represented God. God could not charge Biblical Ethiopians with idol worship because the nation that He selected as priests to make Himself known through (Israel), failed to teach them. So, when Israel failed, God sent judges and prophets to correct them, but they rejected them all.[26] At the last, God sent His son and His son succeeded by creating the path to God for every man through Himself.[27] With the success of Jesus, the practice of worshipping statues that

---

[24] Exodus 19:3-6
[25] Exodus chapter 3
[26] Mark 12:1-11
[27] 1 Timothy 2:5

represented the Supreme Being was no longer accepted by God. Every man, from the time that Jesus resurrected, must come to God through Jesus. So the spirituality of our African ancestors, which was once accepted by God, is no longer accepted. God no longer winks at it as ignorance. The true knowledge of God is in the earth and accessible to every man. It is the responsibility of those who have received and accepted this knowledge to share this knowledge with those that do not know. The message is clear, today God requires every man in every nation to come to Him through Jesus.

II

The Lost Sheep

I am not sent but unto the lost sheep of the house of Israel.
Matthew 15:24

T hus far, I have presented the biblical case for the 'children of the Ethiopians', or indigenous Africans and their descendents as God's other sheep, or God's other chosen people that Jesus spoke of. When I teach these scriptures, I so often get asked this question, "If the Africans are God's people too, then why are they mentioned so few times in the bible while the Jews dominate the written discourse within the pages of the bible?" Jesus gives us the answer to this question, and I will explain it in this chapter, but first let me tell you a little story about an incident that occurred recently that will help provide this explanation.

I currently serve as the Senior Pastor of a progressive community church on the south side of Chicago. I also have on staff an assistant pastor, along with an associate pastor. The assistant pastor is my biological son. The associate pastor is also my son, although not biological. We are the only three people with keys to every door in the facility. The deacons have keys to most doors, but not all. Only the three of us have keys that allow access throughout the facility. Recently, my biological son lost his church keys. He was totally consumed with locating them. He was searching throughout the church, and when people saw him searching, they would ask what he was looking for. He would respond that he was looking for his church keys. He would describe them to people, describe the key ring that they were on, even describe any specific detail that would assist in identifying them. He would be asked where he last used them and he would recount the last time he used them at the church. I remember his mother, my wife, asking him how he was going to get into his home. He responded that his house keys were safe in his pocket; he would then shift the conversation back to his church keys. He was committed to finding his church keys. He never mentioned his house keys to my wife again; all of his conversation was about finding his church keys. When he was asked how he drove to his current location, he would respond that his car keys were safe with him, it was his church keys that he needed to find. He was totally consumed with locating his church keys so they dominated his conversation about his keys. He only spoke of his 'other' keys when they were brought up in the conversation, but even then, he only briefly mentioned them and quickly returned his focus to his lost church keys. Now his house keys, and his car keys, and even his work keys were just as important to him as his church keys, and they served equally critical functions in his life as his church keys, but he only briefly spoke of those keys when prompted, because they were safe with him and he could access them whenever he wanted them. His attention, his conversation, and his focus were solely on his church keys, because those keys were lost.

This paradigm of my son's keys, and how much attention he gave to his lost keys, as opposed to his other keys, provides the perfect example of why the conversation of the Bible is explicitly focused on the Jewish people of Israel and not the 'children of the Ethiopians', even though the 'children of the Ethiopians' are identified as God's other chosen people (we have biblically shown this in the previous chapters of this book). Jesus said *"I am not sent but unto the lost sheep of the house of Israel"*[28] So the sheep of the "house of Israel" were lost. The sheep that are the 'children of the Ethiopians' were **not** lost. Therefore, the 'children of the Ethiopians' are only mentioned in passing, or in other words, they are mentioned only when they are called upon by God to provide the functions for which they were chosen.

This is a bold and powerful statement about the 'house of Israel' as opposed to the 'children of the Ethiopians, but is if fully biblically supported. When Jesus teaches the parable of the lost sheep[29], He shows us how the good shepherd directs His attention to the single lost sheep, and not the ninety-nine sheep that are safe with him. We see this same attention given to the prodigal son that strayed away as opposed to the loyal son that was safe in relationship with his father. In the story of the prodigal son, so much attention was given to the son that strayed that it caused the loyal son

---

[28] Matthew 15:24
[29] Luke 15:3-7

to become jealous. Seeing the jealously in his loyal son, the Father took him aside and assured him that his attention had been focused on the prodigal son because that son separated from him and was out of relationship, but since the loyal son had remained in relationship with him, he always had his attention and everything else that he possessed.

In Biblically Black and Blessed, and again previously in this book, I show that the 'children of the Ethiopians', or indigenous Africans and those that are of African ancestry, have always served the true and living God. So, when Jesus tells the Jewish people that He has other sheep that are not Jewish, then tells them that His father sent Him to the lost sheep of the house of Israel, He is also saying that the other sheep that he mentioned (the children of the Ethiopians) ARE NOT LOST SHEEP!

Western writers, historians, and so-called scholars have consistently portrayed the continent of Africa as a place inhabited by those that worship idol Gods. As I previously stated, this simply is not true. They may have created statures and figures to represent the Supreme Being, but it was the Supreme Being that they were worshipping. And they were worshipping in this manner because they had no knowledge of God. And these African people had no knowledge of God because the nation that God selected to share this knowledge with the world (Israel) failed in performing their duties as priests. And since there can be no transgression of a law without first having that law, God winked at this ignorance.

The failure of Israel as priests necessitated a savior, one that would fulfill the priestly duties that Israel failed to perform for the world.[30] Yeshua, or Jesus is that savior! So, until the resurrection of Jesus, the spirituality and worship of the Supreme Being that was practiced by those of African descent was accepted by God because of their lack of knowledge of Him. As stated earlier, God winked at it, or in plain terms, He overlooked it!

So the 'house of Israel' failed in their assignment and wandered off. They are characterized by God in the Bible as lost sheep. But God's other sheep, the 'children of the Ethiopians' remained in relationship with God, even though knowledge of who God was had not been shared with them, because of the failure of Israel. And each time that God called upon the 'children of the Ethiopians' to come and deliver Israel from their enemies, they responded without hesitation. Examples of their response to God's call are noted by the actions of King Tirhakah, Ebed-melech, and even Queen Makeda (the Queen of Sheba). Truly, God chose the 'children of the Ethiopians, to be the ones that would fight to protect His interests in the earth. They are His warriors, warring against evil and everything that

---

[30] Hebrews 4:14

pronounces itself against the God of all the earth. Just as God chose the 'house of Israel' as His priests, he chose the 'children of the Ethiopians' as His warriors. I will expand on the responsibility that God assigned the 'children of the Ethiopians, vs. the responsibility that God has assigned to the 'house of Israel' in the next chapter.

The 'house of Israel' indeed are God's sheep, but Jesus made it very clear that the 'children of the Ethiopians, are also His sheep, or as He put it, they are His **OTHER SHEEP**!

II

God's Kingdom on Earth

Thy kingdom come.
Thy will be done in earth, as it is in heaven.
Matthew 6:10

I really debated within myself as to whether or not I would write this chapter. I've presented the 'children of the Ethiopians' that are mentioned in Amos 9:7 as the other sheep that Jesus spoke of in John 10:16. It was a daunting task for which I have spent years praying, fasting, reading, studying, and submitting enquiries to God for insight, revelation, and knowledge. Holy Spirit has enabled me to understand things that for years I have sought knowledge. So, concluding the message of this book with this chapter serves as a wrap up, or a pulling together of the data presented and providing insight into God's plan for mankind. The scripture has said in 1 Corinthians 2:16:

> *For who hath known the mind of the Lord, that he may instruct him? But we have the mind of Christ.*

It is beyond our limited abilities to know the mind of God, but when believers enter into relationship with God, we acquire the mind of Christ.[31] And it is with the insight that comes from having the mind of Christ that I write this chapter.

If there is a single failure that I have witnessed in all of my time as a believer, it is this: far too often the Bible is taught as a collection of individual scriptures as opposed to

---

[31] Philippians 2:5

being presented as the complete comprehensive plan of God for mankind. For example, if we comprehend the what, when, and why of Genesis, then we acquire a better understanding of the Apostle Paul's teachings to the Romans, Galatians, etc. When we look beyond a single scripture, chapter, or verse and view each scripture as an interrelated part of God's comprehensive plan, our understanding of events, places, people, struggles, victories, etc. is expanded with clarity. I found this to be so true regarding God's plan for the 'children of the Ethiopians'.

Recently I was led of Holy Spirit to teach my church a series of messages on God's Governance. Little did I know at the time that these messages were just the latest installment in teaching the overall plan of God for mankind. I expounded on God's governance periods on the earth from the very beginning of time, up to today. These governance periods are clearly defined in scripture as

1. Pre-Law direct governance where God governed man by giving instructions directly to individuals. This period spanned from Adam to Moses.[32]
2. The Law -- With Moses, God begin to govern man by providing instruction through written laws that were to be taught and adhered to. This period ranged

---

[32] Romans 5:12-14

from Moses to Samuel.[33] (*The period of governance via the Judges would be within the law*)

3. The Prophets -- With Samuel, we had the beginning of the prophets. Many people don't separate the law and the prophets as distinct governance periods, but Jesus, Paul, and other New Testament writers repeatedly referred to "the law and the prophets", thereby distinguishing them. The governance period of the prophets ranged from Samuel until John the Baptist.[34]

4. The Kingdom of God -- There was brief interlude of God's governance when Jesus was on the earth, but scripture clearly states that with John the Baptist, the governance period of the Kingdom of God begins. It is in this governance period that God governs man via His Holy Spirit that he places within believers. This is the period of God's governance in which we currently reside.[35]

Acknowledging and understanding these periods of God's governance allows us to see clearly that God is a God of order and He has established organizational structure for His created work. When we understand this governance, we can clearly see that all of the preceding governance periods were

---

[33] John 1:16
[34] Luke 16:16
[35] Luke 16:16

meticulously established with the purpose of bringing mankind into the period of the Kingdom of God. The word kingdom is defined as such:

Kingdom -- a politically organized community or major territorial unit having a monarchical form of government headed by a king or queen.

A kingdom has a head, and the subjects of the kingdom have duties and responsibilities as assigned by this head. In the governance period of 'The Kingdom of God', it is clear who sits on the throne as the head. God Himself! And we, the believers, are His subjects and have the assignments and responsibilities that He gives to each of us individually. But the Bible has always grouped people into nations. And as stated earlier, each nation is as a piece of a puzzle that, when combined with the rest of the pieces of the puzzle, create an environment where mankind succeeds in making the world the glorious haven of life that God purposed it to be.

When the disciples asked Jesus to teach them to pray, He first gave them the format for addressing God in prayer. They were to begin by respectfully and reverently addressing God with the understanding that his name is sacred. *"Our father, which art in Heaven, hallowed be thy name"*.[36]

---

[36] Matthew 6:9

After God is appropriately addressed, then the very first petition that Jesus teaches His disciples to make to God is *"Thy kingdom come. Thy will be done in earth, as it is in heaven."*[37]The very first request that Jesus teaches His disciples to make is for God's Kingdom on earth to be established just like it is in heaven. THIS DIRECTLY RELATES TO GOD'S GOVERNANCE! But for us to even comprehend the depth of this request, we first need to have an understanding of just how God's kingdom in heaven is organized and structured. When we know the structure and organization of God's kingdom in heaven, we can better understand what God's plan for humanity on the earth is, even from the very beginning. And when we understand God's purpose and plan for humanity on the earth, we can comprehend the individual assignments that God has tasked the nations on the earth with. But it all begins with understanding the structure of God's kingdom in heaven.

The Kingdom of God in Heaven

Heaven must be an awesome place simply because it is the place where God resides.[38] Jesus even makes this clear when He teaches His disciples how to pray.[39] But in the minds of

---

[37] Matthew 6:10
[38] 1 Kings 8:49
[39] Matthew 6:9

many, Heaven is a quiet, serene, and picturesque place where angels worship and praise all day, where the streets are paved with gold, and the gates in and out of it are made of pearls. We have a mental picture of heaven where no chaos exists, and there are no disruptions to the peace and tranquility that we long for when we get there. Although these picturesque depictions of Heaven are indeed biblical, we should never forget that Heaven is a active and functional kingdom, where God rules as the established head (king) of it. Kingdoms are places where a king or queen rules by implementing their authority and law throughout the land, and when opposition to their rule arises, they defend their kingdom from opposing forces. This is just as true of the Kingdom of Heaven, as that peaceful picturesque place that we desire to make our eternal home. We understand from Bible study that the Kingdom of Heaven has been successfully defended from Lucifer in the past[40], and will continue to be defended with success until the very end[41]. So, just as with earthly kingdoms, there is also opposition to God's Kingdom in Heaven. Heaven's opposition fights against the laws of the Heaven's King (God), and seek to prevent the furtherance of the Kingdom. And at the very core of God's governance, the earth is but an extension of God's authority and rule; and we, the inhabitants of earth, are His

---

[40] Isaiah 14:12-15
[41] Revelations 12:7-9

subjects created to fulfill His will and carry out His purpose in this extension of His Kingdom. This is the reason that Jesus instructed His disciples to pray that God's "kingdom come" and His "will be done" in earth just like it is in Heaven.

It is tempting to continue with our picturesque serene view of heaven, but when opposition arises, Heaven can become a very violent place, and this can occur very quickly. Jesus remarked that He once witnessed Satan being violently evicted from Heaven.[42]   So in order for the king to implement His laws throughout the land, He has to have subjects assigned to specific duties within the organization and structure of the kingdom. Once again, I will challenge the mental picture of Heaven as a place where all that occurs are angels worshipping around the throne, praying and singing while entering the pearly gates, or rejoicing on streets paved with gold. Heaven is a place where the angels have assignments, and those assignments are executed by them in the implementation of God's rule. Sure, there are angels that worship,[43] but there are angels that function in other capacities to secure the kingdom for God, the king. Michael the Archangel is noted throughout the Bible as the leader of God's army of fighters, forever protecting the

---

[42] Luke 10:18
[43] Revelation 5:11-12; Isaiah 6:2-3

Kingdom of Heaven and putting down any and all opposition to the King.[44]Michael is, according to God, a prince and the leader of God's warrior faction of angels stationed in Heaven. And then there's Gabriel. The Bible does not document the responsibilities that Gabriel has, but by function we see that whenever God wanted to send a message to his subjects on earth, Gabriel was the angel tasked to deliver such a message.[45] Gabriel was not only tasked with delivering the message from God, he was also tasked with teaching and explaining the message so that the recipient would have understanding.[46] So it becomes ever so clear that some angels in Heaven function as carriers of God's messages and teachers, when explanation is needed to provide the message recipient with understanding. The Bible shows us that in Heaven, some angels are responsible for singing and praising.[47] It is widely held among believers that the fallen Archangel Lucifer was once tasked with this responsibility before his fall.[48]And we can surmise further that if there are horses in heaven,[49] then some angels must be responsible for maintaining their places of residence (stables), etc. The point that I want to emphasize is that the bible clearly and explicitly states that Heaven is an active

---

[44] Revelation 12:7; Jude 1:9; Daniel 12:1; Daniel 10:13
[45] Luke 1:26; Daniel 8:16; Daniel 9:21;
[46] Daniel 8:16
[47] Job 38:7; Luke 2:13-14
[48] Ezekiel 28:13
[49] Revelation 19:4

functioning kingdom where the angelic inhabitants have assigned responsibilities that secure it and makes it the desirable place where we want to spend eternity. Each order of angels have their specific assignments and responsibilities, that when carried out as God purposed, make them interdependent on each other for the harmonious peaceful functioning of the systems within the Kingdom. As stated earlier, just like a puzzle, each order of angels is indeed unique, but they uniquely fit into the organizational and hierarchical structure that is implemented in the Kingdom of Heaven. At times the angels paths may cross while completing their assignments, but in their day to day responsibilities they may not 'hang out' together. One particular instance where Gabriel's and Michael's path crossed can be found in Daniel when Gabriel was sent to deliver a message to Daniel but was opposed by the Prince of Persia (the Devil). Michael was then sent to assist in getting that message to Daniel. Then after the Prince of Persia was subdued, Gabriel returned to explain the message and its meaning to Daniel.[50] We know from Gabriel's communication with Daniel, that he knew of Michael as a leader (prince) among the angels and that they were on the same team within the Kingdom of God in Heaven. He was well aware that they were serving the same king. This is the organization and structure that Jesus instructed His disciples

---

[50] Daniel 10:12-14

to pray for on earth. When Jesus said to them that they should pray that God's "kingdom come" and that God's "will be done in earth as it is in Heaven", He was instructing them to pray for this Heavenly organization and structure to be established and implemented on earth. Just as God's created beings in Heaven (angels) carry out God's plan in Heaven, Jesus instructed them to pray that God's created beings on earth (man) do likewise here. This would also mean that just as God has assigned to the angels' specific duties, functions, and responsibilities to make Heaven an active functioning kingdom, He has assigned similar duties, functions, and responsibilities of man to establish and implement His kingdom on earth. I will now look at the duties and functions assigned to the nations on the earth (man) that are validated in the Bible either by specific command from God, or by function (noting the duties that they consistently performed for God). Remember Michael's assignment is explicitly stated in the Bible, whereas Gabriel's assignment is extrapolated by noting the functions that he performed within the Kingdom of Heaven's structure. The extent of this book is to highlight the assignment of 'the children of the Ethiopians', so as such is my goal, I will only be looking at the assignments from God to the 'children of the Ethiopians', and the 'house of Israel'.

The Kingdom of God on Earth

When looking at God's assignments to His subjects that are responsible for implementing and fulfilling His purpose, and functioning within His kingdom here on earth, one point must always be at the forefront of any explanation: **God does not deal with us by race, he does not identify us by race, nor does He refer to his earthly creation by race, He identifies us as <u>nations</u>.** So to establish His kingdom here on earth, God created the nations of people and made assignments to these nations, just as we have seen the assignments He made to the angels in His Kingdom in Heaven. One additional point that I will make is that citizenship in either of God's kingdoms is always by choice. God does not force anyone to come under His authority, nor does He force anyone to submit to His governance. Our citizenship in the Kingdom of God is by choice and submission to His authority. This is a decision that all of God's created beings must make. The choice to submit to God's authority has to be made by His created beings in Heaven (the angels), and His created beings here on earth (man). So many times, we don't visualize the angels as having this choice, but remember earlier in this book I mentioned the statement of Jesus that he saw Satan fall from Heaven. Satan, the angel previously known as Lucifer chose not to be a citizen of God's kingdom. He decided that he wanted to overthrow the kingdom and become the king[51]. This did not end very well for him. But he did not get evicted from Heaven alone, as many as a third of the angels that were deceived into following him also lost their citizenship in the Kingdom of Heaven[52].

Considering the assignments to the nations that God purposed to function in His kingdom here on earth, the first nation to be defined is the nation of Israel (*remember I will only be looking at the house of Israel and the children of the Ethiopians in this book*). The fact that Israel has an assignment in God's kingdom on earth is without doubt obvious. Any believer that accepts the Bible as God's word can clearly see, know, and understand the role that the nation of Israel has in the establishment of God's kingdom on earth. They are assigned the responsibilities of priests to deliver, explain, and teach God's laws to the other nations. This is clearly laid out in the bible[53]. To accomplish this, they needed to first know who God is themselves, so they were the first nation to whom God revealed Himself as God. The Ethiopians were inherently serving the Supreme Being, and creating figures to represent the God of whom they had no personal knowledge. As I said earlier, God accepted (*winked at*) the worship of the Ethiopians during this time because

---

[51] Isaiah 14:12-15
[52] Revelation 12:4; Jude 1:6
[53] Exodus 19:7

He had not revealed Himself to them as God. It would be the responsibility of the nation that He assigned the priestly duties within His kingdom on earth, to first to know Him as God, learn of His laws and ways, then deliver this knowledge to the other nations. Simply put, within God's kingdom on earth, the nation of Israel was tasked with learning who God is, then learning the laws of God from God, then teaching God's laws to the other nations of the world. When making a comparison of kingdom responsibilities in Heaven vs. kingdom responsibilities on earth, the nation of Israel are to function in God's kingdom on earth as Gabriel functioned in God's kingdom in Heaven. They were to deliver God's messages and explain them when necessary. They were to be God's ambassadors on the earth.[54] This is an awesome assignment and a critical responsibility within any kingdom. Although Israel's responsibilities in God's kingdom on earth closely align with Gabriel's responsibilities in God's kingdom in Heaven, their assignment is documented in scripture, as Michael the Archangel's is. But as I previously stated, the nation of Israel failed in their responsibility. Their failure consequently impacted the other nations of the world in a very negative way. Their failure as priests meant that knowledge of God, as God, did not make it to the children of the Ethiopians. And because of this, they continued to create statues of stone, stick, stubble, etc. to represent the

---

[54] 2 Corinthians 5:20

Supreme Being and God continued to accept their worship because they yet had no knowledge of Him as God. The impact of Israel's failure was more devastating for the gentile nations. For as priests, they were responsible for reconnecting the gentiles with God. So you can see that the failure of Israel as God's priests within God's kingdom on earth had enormous negative impact on the earth. But God had the fix for their failure. Jesus is this fix. God divinely and meticulously orchestrated the entrance of Jesus into this world in such a way that Jesus would replace the nation of Israel as God's priest in His kingdom on earth. He did this by bringing Jesus into the earth in the lineage of Judah of the nation of Israel, but without giving Him earthly genetics that emanate from a father. With this miraculous entry into the world and a life that was the perfect example of man; Jesus could share His knowledge of who the Supreme Being is with the children of the Ethiopians while providing access for the gentiles to re-connect with God. With knowledge of God as God now available, God no longer winked at the Ethiopians worshipping Him by creating statues that represented the Supreme Being; and access to re-connect with God meant that any excuse for not acknowledging God was taken away from the gentiles. Therefore, the assignment to the nation of Israel within God's kingdom on earth is by biblical command and it is clear, they are to function as God's priests upon the face of this earth.

But it takes more than one function to successfully maintain a kingdom. God's kingdom on earth would not be complete if the only assignment to the nations were that Israel are the priests. Remember that in God's kingdom in Heaven, assignments are made for those that will carry God's messages, those that will protect the kingdom from opposition, those that will worship, etc. So the other nation that I will discuss their Godly assignment in God's kingdom on earth is the 'children of the Ethiopians', or the Africans. Like the nation of Israel, the assignment given to the 'children of the Ethiopians' is also very clear in the bible. But like Gabriel, there is no biblical reference that states what their assignment is, so just as we did with Gabriel, we will examine the functions that God commanded them to perform, and with knowledge of these functions, we will extrapolate their assignment. The first function that I will examine is the mission that God sent them on in 2 Kings chapter 19. Isaiah was the prophet in Jerusalem at the time so this mission is also recorded on Isaiah chapter 37. Judah was under attack by the Assyrian nation and things did not look good. And when death and destruction appeared to be the certain outcome for Israel, God sent King Tirhakah from Ethiopia with his Ethiopian armies to deliver Israel[55]. Whenever I read this, I am reminded of the time that God sent Michael the warrior angel to assist Gabriel the

---

[55] 2 Kings 19:9; Isaiah 37:9

messenger angel because the fight that Gabriel found himself in with the Prince of Persia was a bit much for him. But King Tirhakah, and his Ethiopian army, is not the only example for which we see the children of the Ethiopians functioning in their God assigned purpose within God's kingdom on earth, let's take a look at the actions of Ebed-melech, the Ethiopian Eunuch, and how God sent him to rescue the prophet Jeremiah from death.[56] In both of these instances, the Ethiopians were sent by God and they stood up to fight for justice in God's kingdom here on earth. In this we see the warrior function that God assigned to Michael in His kingdom in Heaven being performed by the 'children of the Ethiopians' in His Kingdom on earth. We even see this in Makeda, the Queen of Sheba (Ethiopia) as God sent her up from her African home to validate Solomon to the world. She came up, gave Solomon an exam to test his wisdom, and when he met her criteria, she supported him and announced him to the world![57]Although not as explicitly clear as the other instances, one may conclude that Moses' selection of an Ethiopian woman for a wife at a time when a very young nation of Israel faced it most formidable enemies also indicate that Moses understood the assignment that God made to the 'children of the Ethiopians'. The Bible is very clear regarding the Ethiopians; they are God's people that

---

[56] Jeremiah 38:7-13
[57] I Kings 10:1-10

are called to be the warriors on the earth. Their assignment has them fighting for justice and righteousness in the face of opposing evil. Anyone needing further proof of God's assignment to the Ethiopians within His kingdom on earth need look no further than the attempts to colonize the African continent in the late 1800's. In the Berlin Conference of 1885, the European nations held a series of meetings to divide the entire continent of Africa among them. Prior to this, the whole of Africa below the Sahara was commonly known as Ethiopia. This is the Biblical Ethiopia that I referenced earlier in this book. In this conference in Berlin, they decided which portions of Africa each European nation would get and colonize. It was at this time that the boundaries of Ethiopia as we know it today were drawn. It was determined in this Berlin conference that Italy would get current day Ethiopia. But Ethiopia stood and fought for their freedom, their independence, and their right to submit only to the King who would establish His kingdom here on earth. That king is God. So being outnumbered, overpowered, outgunned, and under-resourced physically, these Ethiopian warriors beat back the Italians numerous times. Eventually the Italians ceased trying to take this country. This left Ethiopia as the only African nation on the continent to successfully resist their oppressors. When you consider how their victory was possible, it could only be that they were functioning in their assignment within the Kingdom of God on earth. Both the Bible and secular history attest to the

Ethiopian people as warriors and the Bible makes it clear that this is their assignment within the Kingdom of God on earth.

So once we understand that by creating earth and populating it with the nations of the earth, God was expanding His kingdom. And just as He did not force the inhabitants of His Kingdom in Heaven to submit, but rather judged those that did not[58]; He does not force the inhabitants on earth to submit. Submission to the king (God) is an individual choice. This is why the first petition that Jesus teaches His disciples to make to God when praying is *"Thy kingdom come. Thy will be done on earth as it is in heaven."* The children of the Ethiopians are instrumental in God's Kingdom coming (being establishing) on earth, like it is in heaven!

[58] Jude 1:6

II

CONCLUSION

And other sheep I have, which are not of this fold: them also I must bring, and they shall hear my voice; and there shall be one fold, and one shepherd.

John 10:16

I will conclude this book by showing how important it is for both the 'children of Israel' and the 'children of the Ethiopians' to step up and perform the duties that have been assigned to us within God's Kingdom on the earth. If Jesus' prayer is to be answered, these two nations must begin functioning in their kingdom assignments. There are numerous similarities between these two nations, and that is to be expected, because these two nations are clearly identified in the Bible as nations selected for specific assignments in God's kingdom on the earth. And because of their divine selection, they must deal with similar attacks from the opposition. This is validated and verified throughout the annals of history as well as in the pages of the Bible. I will briefly examine one major event that highlights the similarities in the opposition that each nation faced.

Jewish Holocaust

This horrific event is recorded in every historical catalogue known to man. In the Jewish Holocaust, evil forces under the leadership of Adolf Hitler and acting in opposition to God, attempted to annihilate the entire nation of Israel. History has it recorded that during this period of extreme hate, violence, and genocide against the Jewish people, more than six million Jews were horrifically slaughtered. This was obviously an attempt by Satan to terminate the nation that

God selected to be His priests on earth and thereby prevent the kingdom of God from being established on earth as it is in heaven. But even through the suffering, God is faithful and the Jewish nation remains to this day.

African Holocaust

Though not as highly publicized and taught in history as the Jewish Holocaust, the African Holocaust is equally appalling, more horrific, and had millions more victims than the Jewish Holocaust. While attempting to take the continent, King Leopold and his Belgium murderers slaughtered more than ten million of the 'children of the Ethiopians' in the African Congo. Although this is known to the world, it is not taught in history classes, nor remembered with memorials; neither is any time set aside in solemnity to pray for the descendents of the victims. Knowing that the assignment that God issued to the 'children of the Ethiopians, and knowing that Jesus instructions were to pray that God's Kingdom be established on earth like it is in Heaven, and understanding that this kingdom establishment required the 'children of the Ethiopians' to function as warriors for truth and justice, Satan made an attempt to destroy God's fighting force on earth before they could walk in their kingdom assignment. But God is yet faithful because the 'children of the Ethiopians' and their descendants remain until today.

I could continue with the persecutions and subsequent dispersion of the nation of Israel by Nebuchadnezzar, Greece, or the Romans; I could then liken that persecution to the persecution and subsequent dispersion of the 'children of the Ethiopians' by the Greece, Belgium, Britain, etc. The similarities of their persecution are remarkable for two primary reasons, (1) they share the same opposition; (2) the motive of their opposition has always been the same; this singular motive has been, is, and will always be **to prevent the establishment of the kingdom of God on earth like it is in Heaven**.

Although the world consists of a diverse array of people that are of different nations with different backgrounds, the fact that we all are children of God brings us together like nothing else. Our differences are not weaknesses; neither do these differences elevate any people over the others. Our differences should represent the differences in our Godly assignment and purpose in the earth. And just like any one unique piece of a puzzle is needed to complete that puzzle, each distinct individual nation is also needed to complete the earth. The uniqueness of who we are comes from God for the purpose of making this world a better place. God created us as such so that the only way that the world can exist in peaceful harmonious growth and achieve worldly success, is that we come together and work in unison, fulfilling our God assigned responsibilities. When we do this, God's kingdom will be established on earth, just like it is in Heaven. It is then that the world will experience the answer to the prayer that Jesus instructed His disciples to pray in St. Matthew chapter 6, verse 10:

Thy kingdom come. Thy will be done in earth, as it is in heaven.

God Bless!

Notes

Notes

www.ingramcontent.com/pod-product-compliance
Lightning Source LLC
Chambersburg PA
CBHW051544120626
46551CB00013B/1362